JOYISM

THE ART OF RECLAIMING JOY DAILY TO LIVE A MORE PURPOSE DRIVEN LIFE

AUTHOR CARRIE WOODEN - THE JOY COACH

© **Copyright Carrie Wooden 2022 - All rights reserved.**

The content contained within this book may not be reproduced, duplicated or transmitted without direct written permission from the author or the publisher.

Under no circumstances will any blame or legal responsibility be held against the publisher, or author, for any damages, reparation, or monetary loss due to the information contained within this book. Either directly or indirectly. You are responsible for your own choices, actions, and results.

Legal Notice:

This book is copyright protected. This book is only for personal use. You cannot amend, distribute, sell, use, quote or paraphrase any part, or the content within this book, without the consent of the author or publisher.

Disclaimer Notice:

Please note the information contained within this document is for educational and entertainment purposes only. All effort has been executed to present accurate, up to date, and reliable, complete information. No warranties of any kind are declared or implied. Readers acknowledge that the author is not engaging in the rendering of legal, financial, medical or professional advice. The content within this book has been derived from various sources. Please consult a licensed professional before attempting any techniques outlined in this book.

By reading this document, the reader agrees that under no circumstances is the author responsible for any losses, direct or indirect, which are incurred as a result of the use of the information contained within this document, including, but not limited to, — errors, omissions, or inaccuracies.

CONTENTS

Foreword   5
Introduction   7

1. What is Joy?   11
2. How do I know it is Joy?   19
3. Joyism?   29
4. What are our words Saying?   37
5. What are you thinking?   47
6. Emotions: Your Compass   59
7. What do you Believe?   67
8. Ready, Set, and Go…   75
9. Wrapping it up with a bow!   83
10. Sharing Joy   85

Acknowledgments   107

FOREWORD

Joy is such an amazing and sometimes elusive emotion it can be found in the most life-changing positive situation and is also present in the simplest of moments. So, what is joy and how can you harness this beautiful emotion?

Throughout this book and in her work as a Joy Coach Carrie guides you through exactly what to do to embody joy in your daily life.

In my own joy experience, I discovered that you cannot detach and disassociate from pain, sadness, heartache and stress without also losing your connection to joy. This, I believe, is at the crux of why so many people lack the true feeling of joy in their lives. It is a choice. A choice to feel the full gamut of emotions every day, good and the bad.

So how can you feel this range of human emotions and move through the discomforting ones so you can remain in that joyous life affirming state?

Let Carrie take you on this beautiful joy journey and you will be amazed at the benefits you will walk away with.

Ultimately, to me, joy is synonymous with true personal power and embodiment. So, here is to you, may you find joy, be joy and spread joy throughout your life.

Jessica Shada

INTRODUCTION

Welcome friend Reclaiming your joy is one of the greatest gifts you can give yourself and others, and who doesn't like great gifts! It is time to invest in you by doing something for yourself.

Where did your joy go? Have you ever wondered what happened to the joy-filled life you used to live? Have we let the day-to-day busyness of life drain us of all our joy? Do you want your joy back? Who wouldn't say yes to those questions? I personally cannot think of anyone who doesn't want a joy-filled life! Reclaiming your joy is the greatest gift you can give yourself and others. This moment is all you have; you can recall the past and dream of the future but now is where you are. The now moment is where we live. This book will help you in practical ways to reclaim the joy that is who you are, who you were created to be. So, let's get this party started!

Long, long ago in a galaxy far, far away…. (Giggling to myself). Just kidding, not too long ago on planet Earth, I found myself questioning how my life had become a joyless experience. I was checking off all the boxes of who I was raised to be, who I believed at the time I was supposed to be, and who I thought others needed me to be. I was super busy with doing all the stuff in my life, but joy did not seem to be present anymore. To make a long joyless story short, I had become an over-giving overachiever trying to make sure everybody else's needs were met with no thought of my own needs, dreams, or desires. Who here can relate? I know I sure can! The tipping point or Ah-ha moment for me was during a plane ride, to help a friend of course, where I finally realized that I was just as important as everyone else and needed to put the oxygen mask on first. You can't give from an empty cup or if you are passed out on the floor. So, my journey to find and reclaim my joy started.

Throughout this book, I will share lessons I have learned, processes and activities to help you on your way and a good laugh or two, possibly more. I have reclaimed my joy and found my soul purpose: now it is your turn.

I am a Joy Bringer. I am "The Joy Coach," and my desire for this book is to help the over-giving overachievers out there who have lost their joy along the way to realize they are co-creators in this 3D journey, and joy can be chosen daily! Let your journey to joy start now. You are worth it.

"Sometimes in life, we become so focused on the finish line that we fail to find the Joy in the Journey."

— DIETER F UCHTDORF

WHAT IS JOY?

"Joy is an echo of the creator in Us"

Let us first look at what the Merriam-Webster dictionary has to say about all this.

Joy as a Noun

1. The emotion evoked by well-being, success, or good fortune or by the prospect of possessing what one desires: Delight
2. The expression or exhibition of such emotion: Gaiety

    a. A state of happiness or felicity: Bliss
    b. A source of delight

Joy as a Verb

1. To experience great pleasure of delight: Rejoice

Here are a couple of quotes that also define Joy

> *"Joy is the serious business of Heaven"*
>
> — C.S. LEWIS

> *"Joy is prayer; joy is strength, joy is love, joy is a net of love by which you can catch souls"*
>
> — MOTHER TERESA

Time to Ponder Activity

What is your definition of Joy? Everyone has a different perspective on what joy is for them. Write down the first thing that comes to mind, then ponder on joy and continue adding to your definition…

✎…

✎…

✎…

My favorite definition of Joy is *"Joy is the Soul of Happiness"* **Robert Holden PhD**

When you consider this definition what comes to mind for you? What thoughts, beliefs or feelings arise for you? Take a moment and jot down your thoughts…

✎…

✎…

✎…

The question often comes up, "Isn't joy and happiness the same thing?" The answer to that question is no, nada, and nope. Let us compare the two and ponder on the difference.

Happiness is an emotion that comes and goes with external things. For example, more money, a new car or truck if that is what you prefer, a exotic vacation, or even a piece of cheesecake (raspberry white chocolate works for me). It tends to be triggered and generally based on other people, places, things, thoughts, and events. Feelings range from satisfaction to intense pleasure and anywhere in between. It is more of an outward expression that is generally temporary. Happiness is caused or chosen from a variety of experiences. Happiness is about one's self-pleasure.

On the other hand, Joy is a stronger state of being that results in contentment and inner peace. The feeling you had on your wedding day, the birth of a child, or the peace of being still in nature. Joy is lasting and based on inward circumstances. Serving others with no expectation of personal gain brings about joy. Feeling close to and connected to your creator can bring joy. Joy my not always be about oneself but be about others' contentment also.

Joy is also one of those unique emotions/experiences that can be felt simultaneously with other feelings or emotions. For example, when my children's father passed away, there were buckets of sadness and tears but also joy in remembering all the amazing things and events that we shared with him previously. The belief we hold that we will see him again also brings the knowingness of joy.

"Joy is not in things. It is in us."

— BENJAMIN FRANKLIN

Happiness does no bring joy. Joy is not a by-product of happiness. Joy is infused with peace and comfort. Joy is an inner feeling, and inner knowing. Does this make sense to you? Are we still on the same page?

<u>Time to Ponder Activity</u>

Let us create you list of Joy vs. Happiness

List five examples of what brings you Joy

1.

2.

3.

4.

5.

List five examples of what bring you Happiness

1.

2.

3.

4.

5.

Hellen Keller described joy as *"the holy fire that keeps purpose warm and our intelligence aglow."*

Can you see how this resonates in the items that are listed under what brings you joy? Joy is more than just an emotion or state of mind; it is more profound. I love hearing the ideas and thought of children and young adults. Listed below are some definitions of joy unedited from the minds of the young and young at heart…

A Collection of Joy definitions from the younger generations

(And a few grown men that wanted to add their two cents)

- *"Joy is just bigger than happiness"* Madelyn, age 8
- *"Joy is fishing everyday"* Mason, age 9
- *"PEANUT BUTTER!!"* Addalyn age 3
- *"Playing makes me have joy"* Rohnan, age 4
- *"Joy means to learn something"* Kasen age 6
- *"It means happiness and fun"* Merrick, age 8
- *"Having fun, something that makes me happy. Reading, having friend to play with, and doing crafts"* Kaylee age 9
- *"When you are genuinely happy, not faking it"* Phoebe age 17
- *"Feeling that improves my mood and makes me want to do stuff. Isn't if have something to do with chemical stuff in your brain?"* Joaquin, age 10
  Note: this child plans on being an astronaut
- *"Excitement, cars and girls"* Diego, age 17
- *"My brothers"* Jaxon, age 7
- *"Playing games, like a frisbee with mom and dad"* Rylee, age 6
- *"I don't know"* Cedar, age 13
- *"Umm playing on my phone...."* Ella, age 11
- *"Playing in nature"* Cybil, age 7

- Conner, age 5 ran in the other direction when asked what his thoughts were.
- Jackson, age 2 just kept repeating the word Joy over and over.
- *"My crazy family"* Travis, age 42 years young
- *"Doing nice things for other people"* Gwen, age 9
- *"Doing what I love, like draw, be alone, listen to music, read, write and play video games"* Ruby, age 10
- *"Camping"* Ryder, age 8
- *"Feeling my soft blanket when I go to sleep"* Annie, age 4
- *"Joy is a girl's name…oh, joy is grilled cheese and tomato soup"* Michael, age 57 years young
- *"If you don't know, then you might need to go back to homeschooling"* Hunter, age 7
- *"Cuddling with my puppy"* Jackie, age 4
- *"Be happy. I'm happy because I go to my cousin's house"* Nannette, age 5
- *"For me joy is feeling of happiness which I feel when something good or nice happens to me. i.e: seeing my family or being with my friends after a long time."* Mya, age 11

2

HOW DO I KNOW IT IS JOY?

In the last chapter, we experienced joy through an amusing list of what the younger generation defines joy as, so let us look at what you believe joy is, what brings you joy and/or what gives you joy.

Review what you listed in the last chapter as examples of joy. As you read what you had written down, think about going a little deeper with each instance. Contemplate each one. As you go deeper, I bet you will notice a smile or two crossing your face!

<u>Time to Ponder Activity</u>

Now pick the most joyful experience from your **childhood** and write it out including as much detail as you can remember. Can you describe the experience with all five of your senses? What did you hear, smell, taste, touch and see in this experience?

✎…

✎…

✎…

✎…

✎…

✎…

✎…

✎…

✎…

✎…

✎…

Now choose an experience of joy from your **Teen years**. For me, this one was a challenge as the teenage years were a crazy time where I was just trying to figure life out and where I fit in. Describe your experience in as much detail as you can possibly remember…

Note: if you are thinking "Carrie, I don't know" well think of it this way, if you had to pick something, what would it be? You won't be graded on this I promise.

✎…

✎…

✎…

✎…

✎…

✎…

✎…

✎…

✎…

✎…

✎…

✎…

✎…

✎…

Next, choose the best or favorite experience of joy from your life now as an adult. This is generally where remembering an experience is a bit easier. Describe with as much detail as you can…

✎...

✎...

✎...

✎...

✎...

✎...

✎...

✎...

✎...

✎...

✎...

✎...

✎...

Okay, now that you have your examples and experiences written down, how do they make you feel? Sit a moment with each feeling as they come up, do not judge any of the feelings. Relish in the emotions of Joy. Not like pickle relish but more like appreciation or taking pleasure in. Write down your feelings here...

Feelings from your childhood memory

✏️...

✏️...

✏️...

Feelings from your young adult(teenage) memory

✏️...

✏️...

✏️...

Feelings from your Adult memory

✏️...

✏️...

✏️...

I was chatting about joy with my good friend Toni as she recalled that swimming underwater upstream in the local river is what brought her joy when she was young. She talked about how that experience as a child was her happy place. It brought her joy as a child and as an adult. It was in this moment where she was able to reconnect and reclaim her joy. She lit up as she described the experience to me with incredible detail. She smiled as she described how the water felt and how much fun she had each time she went to the river. She also talked about sharing this joy with her granddaughter recently when she took her to swim in the river, of course underwater and upstream. This made their connection such a memorable one.

"Joy is increased by spreading it to others."

— ROBERT MURRAY MCCHEYNE

What thought come to your mind when you review your list? There are no right or wrong answers here. Thoughts are essential as we will cover in greater detail in chapter 5

✎…

✎…

✎…

How do the examples you have had in your childhood and youth differ from the examples from your adulthood? What is the common thread between them? What are the differences if there are any?

✎…

✎…

✎…

"Joy is only as far away as you place it."

What if I told you, you could call in the energy or feeling of joy anytime you desired to? Hooray!!! You Can! As you have already felt joy in your life before this very moment, you can choose to feel it anytime you wish.

<u>Time to Ponder Activity</u>

This next activity or exercise is adapted from The Council of Light channeled by Christy Whitman

Try this out. Recall your most joyful experience, and this could be when you were young playing in muddy puddles, reconnection with an old friend or when you met the love of your life, traveling to a distant land that you had dreamed about for years, or maybe even the birth of a child.

When you bring this experience to mind, start to feel the joy grow. Expand on the details in your mind until you feel joy, and as you begin to feel it grow in your heart center, focus your attention on that feeling. Now, as you breathe in, imagine bringing more of that feeling into your body. Breathe in joy and breathe out any resistance or negative emotions you might be holding onto or that you do not want. Feel the joy as deeply as you can and then imagine that feeling expanding to fill your entire body, every single cell. See how expanded you can make this feeling of joy. Imagine you can fill the room you are in with this energy. What about filling the house you are in, then the city, state, and country? Can you imagine expanding it to cover the planet? When you have expanded the feeling of joy as much as you can imagine, slowly bring your awareness back into the room you are in.

Note: Closing your eyes during this exercise will help you to focus more easily. Figured if I told you to close your eyes at the beginning of this exercise, it might be hard to read what you were supposed to be doing.

How easy or difficult was this exercise for you? How far were you able to expand your Joy? On a scale from 1 to 10 how much joy were you able to feel? Practicing this exercise will make bringing joy into your life easier.

1 2 3 4 5 6 7 8 9 10

Joy is beyond time and Space.

One of the Ah-ha moments for me on knowing what joy is to me personally came in a session with Christy Whitman and The Quantum Council of Light. She taught us and brought to our awareness that everything is subjective. So, what is an amazing experience for me might not be that way for you. Let me explain subjectivity better with an exercise Christy took us through

The Blue Car Exercise

In this exercise, you close your eyes (read the paragraph before closing your eyes) and think of a blue car. Can you see that blue car? If you don't like blue you can pick a different color: the color doesn't matter. The blue car that you imagine might be very different than the blue car I have imagined. I might be thinking of an old blue four-door rambler with rusty fenders sitting in a field of oats, and you might be thinking of a brand ne shiny superman blue BMW sitting in your garage, can you smell the "new" car smell? Just a little bit of a difference between the two of those images. You attuned your awareness to the car. I only suggested a blue care, you are the one who thought of it.

Can you see how your experience vs. mine is different/subjective? How boring would life be if everyone had the same experience or liked the exact same thing! Yay for variety in life. That old blue rambler was my family's car when I was about eight years old. There were lots of fun road trip memories tied to it. So even though I could pick any blue vehicle, this is the one that always comes to mind first. So, when you thought of your blue car, what was your reason? Is there Joy attached to that thought?

This exercise allows you to align with the blue car and we will go into more detail on the importance of alignment regarding reclaiming your joy in the next chapter. Which would be, your guessed it chapter three... We are just moving right along now, aren't we?

Time to Ponder Activity

Now that we understand a bit more on everything being subjective write down three ways you now know "how it is Joy" ...

1.

2.

3.

> *"The joy we feel has little to do with the circumstances of our lives and everything to do with the focus of our lives."*
>
> — RUSSEL M NELSON

3

JOYISM?

HOW DO I RECLAIM MY JOY?

So, you want to know how to reclaim your joy? You have come to the right place. And with the activities we have been working through, you are well on the path!

> *"Learning to live in the present moment is part of the pat of Joy."*
>
> — SARA BAN BREATHNACH

Let us start by figuring out what keeps you from living a life filled with joy consistently. Often it is easier to understand what we want by knowing what it is we do not want. We have talked about what joy is and how we know if we have it, so what is stealing your joy?

Time to Ponder Activity

List the top 4 things that you think or feel steals your joy? Honestly, there are no right or wrong answers here either, or you probably could list more, but let us just list your top four...

Example: rude people

1.

2.

3.

4.

Okay, I did not give you tons of space to write because we do not want to dwell in the negative energy of the lack of joy and the things that take it away from us. We are here to reclaim it! Focusing on the lack will only bring you more lack.

Those things that you have stated steal your joy are or could be some of your triggers. Being aware of this will help you on your journey to reclaiming your joy filled life. The more awareness you have the easier it is going to be to sidestep the pitfalls on your joy journey.

In correlation to the four items listed above, let's lost why you allow yourself to be robbed of you with these things. What is it about these that have the power to steal your joy? Yes, I might just be implying that you have control over what triggers you...

Example: rude people, I feel that everyone should be kinder or think before they open their mouths, it is not my fault they are having issues.

1.

2.

3.

4.

What if instead of getting triggered by x, y, and z you got curious instead. Let's take for example, the rude people. What if the rude person is only someone having a horrible day due to unforeseen circumstances that you are not aware of? What if that rude person just lost their job or they received terrible news from the doctor? What if they just had a relationship fall apart? What if they stubbed their toe or their ice cream fell on the ground?

When you get curious, it opens you up to seeing that perhaps their rudeness has absolutely nothing to do with you and everything to do with them. Take a moment and think of a situation where something didn't go your way, might there have been any part of this event that you could get curious about? Are you getting curious? Awesome, I knew you could do it!

Do you know what that means? It means you can in this moment or any other moment that may come along and make it an opportunity to spread your joy. How powerful is it to receive a smile from a stranger or even a simple compliment? "Your hair looks nice today. I love your outfit." Have you ever been the person having a bad day, and out of the blue, someone smiles at you, or you receive a call from an old friend wondering how you have been, allowing you to feel seen and validated?

This joy inside of us is an untapped reservoir of potential. How does it feel when others share their joy with you? Write down an example from your life in which someone shared joy with you. Consider how things could have been different if you had not experienced this at that moment in time…

✎…

✎…

✎…

✎…

Next question

In What ways can you share your joy with others today? What is your go to things to share joy…

✎…

✎…

✎…

Now let's talk about what it even means to reclaim something.

The definition of reclaim is to restore to a previous natural state.

What if your joy can not be taken from you? What if you have just forgotten that your joy is a part of who you are and were created to be. Joy is your natural state. What if you having been made in the image of God/Source/Divine, which is pure positive energy, are an extension of that energy? Would that not mean that love and joy are your birthrights?

Guess what? You are created from precisely this source energy! I am sure even aliens are made from source energy. They too can experience joy! Everything is energy.

Time to Ponder Activity

Ponder on the following statements, since we are reclaiming or restoring something that previously existed.

Joy is constant and always with us; it is quiet and invisibly always present, and everywhere we are.

Joy is a natural state of being.

Do these statements feel true to you?

Tell me, what about these two stated ideas regarding the nature of joy resonates with you? What resistance, if any do you have?

✎...

✎...

✎...

Let's talk about alignment, it really is the secret sauce!

The key to reclaiming your joy is alignment. Yep, it means energetically getting your ducks in a row, but some of you may say, "Carrie I don't have ducks; I have squirrels!" that is okay, too; it just might take a little more practice and imagination to line them up. This perfect state of alignment is who you really are, who your higher self and God/Source/Divine designed you to be. Christy Whitman's life-changing book, The Desire Factor channeled by the Council of Light, explains how this step of alignment may be more difficult for many folks because there are always ways to go deeper with it. The great part is that our emotions are our personal navigation system! When we are out of alignment, we feel bad; when we are in alignment, we feel good.

How easy is that. Another awesome part is that you have 100% complete power to choose to re-align if you are out of alignment. We all are a little of sometimes. Yes, there is that responsibility thing yet again.

I absolutely love the following quote from The Quantum Council of Light in which sums up alignment beautifully.

> *"Alignment is the key to everything you desire. If you are not connected to the power source from which the desire came, you are out there trying, willing, and forcing your desires into form. You are divinely designed to thrive and feel good, and that means your desires are an extension of the alignment to your source"*
>
> — THE QUANTUM COUNCIL OF LIGHT

Christy teaches about the five aspects of alignment consciousness, which are... drum roll, please...

1. Your words
2. Your thoughts
3. Your Emotions/feelings
4. Your Beliefs/perspectives
5. Your Actions

She explains how the words we speak, the thoughts we choose to think, the beliefs/perspective we are holding, the emotions we are or are not feeling and the actions we choose to take all must be in alignment. In the next five chapters we are going to dive deeper with each of these aspects separately in relation to reclaiming your Joy.

4

WHAT ARE OUR WORDS SAYING?

Have you ever stopped to think about this? We have all heard the saying that words can destroy, and words can create, so what are you creating or destroying with your words? Well, in this book, we will be creating an awesome amount of joy in our daily lives! Are you ready?

"Good words are worth much and cost little."

— GEORGE HERBERT

Let us talk about the power of words. Can you remember back in your life or even just today when someone complimented you? How did that feel? Did a smile come across your face? What about someone criticizing something you did or didn't do? How did that feel: How words are used also affects our joy levels. For example, the word perfect can bring joy or destroy it. "That cake you made for the party was perfect" versus "Make sure the cake is perfect, so no one is disappointed," see the difference? Feel the difference? One is an uplifting comment and the other has a sense of stress that goes along with it. I no not know anyone who can feel joy when they are stressed out and worrying about letting someone down, do you?

Words do not even have to be spoken to have an impact on our lives. For example, how does it feel when you see a shirt or sign that says, "Life is Good"? Did a smile come across your face as you imagined seeing that? What about a shirt or sign that says, "I'm Grumpy" How does that feel? We are inundated with words on television, on billboards, and even notices in the mail. Words are everywhere. The good news is you get to choose how you respond to those words. You get to choose the words that you want to use daily.

Choose your words wisely, for a whole Joy-filled life is waiting for you!

Words have been found even to affect water crystals and because our bodies are approximately sixty percent water, do you think it might be essential to watch your words? Dr. Masaru Emoto conducted experiments on water molecules. The experiments showed that words, thoughts and intentions can physically alter the structure of the water crystals. He found that words that were positive, loving and encouraging would create unique symmetric crystals. While on the other hand, the words that were angry, hateful and discouraging did just the opposite.

Dr. Emoto demonstrated that words have a vibration and will alter the structure of water crystals. He found that uplifting, positive and encouraging words created beautiful, balanced, and symmetric crystals. Destructive, hateful and evil words had the opposite effect on the water crystals. The visual evidence is quite powerful. There are quite a few videos on youtube if you are interested in checking this out.

So, what words will bring you joy? Remember that your "joy" words and mine might be different.

Time to Ponder Activity

Let's make a list of the words you might be using and words that might be new to you; who doesn't love learning new words? First make a list of any word or phrases that bring you joy and make you smile; you can put these on the left side. On the right side list the words you notice yourself using that might bring your energy down or the energy of others. Thake your time with this and even add to your lists over the next few days. There is no rush. Remember that there are no right or wrong answers. These lists will help in your awareness of the words that are coming out of your mouth.

> *"Words have power; words are power; words could be your power also."*
>
> — MOHAMMED QAHTANI

Joyful words

Example: excited, rainbows

✎...

✎...

✎...

Words that are NOT Joyful

Example: work, I can't, tuff

✎...

✎...

✎...

How did your list turn out? Was one side of the list easier that the other? Our words have the power not only to impact others around us but ourselves also. What words did you notice take away from your daily joy? What words made you feel so much joy you just kept repeating them to yourself?

What about the word supercalifragilisticexpialidocious? Now that word can definitely bring a smile to your face! That word has the power to bring a song to mind. It is okay you can sing it; I know you want to!

Have you ever noticed when a child loves how a word sounds, they just keep repeating it over and over? Which depending on the word, can bring a smile to your face also. A four-year-old loudly repeating the word poop every two seconds might not bring you joy if you are in the grocery store, but then again, it might just make laughter fill your ears. Just saying.

Now that you have your list filled in pick your favorite "Joy" word and see how often you can use it. You might even repeat your "Joy" word out loud or to yourself, in the car or the grocery store. Repeating your "Joy" word especially when you start feeling out of sorts or out of alignment.

> *"Don't mix bad words with your bad mood. You will have many opportunities to change a mood, but you can not replace the words you have spoken."*
>
> — UNKNOWN

Now that you are more aware of the words you are using, you can control how you use them Are you going to use your word power for good or evil? A single kind word can change someone's entire day.

Time for Ponder Activity

With this activity, you choose whether you will do it for a set time or a set amount of people. For the next set amount of time or people you will be sharing your joy-filled words with. These words can be in the form of a spoken compliment, a written note, or even a sign you put up at your desk at work. Get creative in sharing your joy words. Speaking random words at people in the grocery store could be awkward, but it might bring joy to someone needing those joy filled words.

Notice how others are affected by this activity, notice how you are affected by doing this also. Find the joy in the moment. Have fun with it.

Journal below your experiences as you do this activity, taking not of the amount of joy that you are able to create, not only for yourself but others around you.

✎...

✎...

✎...

✎...

✎...

✎...

✎...

✎...

✎...

✎...

✎...

✎...

✎...

Speak of Joy and watch it expand!

I love the quote by N. Scott Momaday that says, *"If you believe in the power of words, you can bring about physical changes in the universe."*

Ponder on that for a moment. What kind of changes can you bring about in the universe? What types of changes do you want to bring about? If that seems too big of a space, what about just in your life, in your home, or in your workspace? What would change for you if you only spoke of joy? How would you be different? How would others respond differently to you? Is that a reality you would like to line in? Remember joy shared has a ripple effect in the universe.

Describe your life if this was the case…

✎…

✎…

✎…

✎…

✎…

✎…

✎…

✎…

✎…

✎…

✎…

Here is a list of some synonyms and other words for Joy

- amusement
- bliss
- charm
- elation
- wonder
- gaiety
- cheer
- comfort
- glee
- humor
- satisfaction
- pride
- ecstasy
- hilarity
- gladness
- frolic
- festivity
- liveliness
- solace
- merriment
- luxury
- refreshing
- treasure
- treat

- rejoicing
- jubilance
- revelry
- enchanting
- felicities
- blessed
- heaven
- euphoria
- paradise
- cool
- excitement
- rhapsody
- expansiveness

Joy Affirmations (words)

- I choose only words of joy
- I say positive things to myself and others
- My words bring joy always
- I express joy through the power of my words
- My communication with others is joyful
- I am Joy

5

WHAT ARE YOU THINKING?

"Words are the clothes thoughts wear"

— **SAMUEL BECKETT**

I believe this quote by Samuel Beckett sums up what words are, and it brings us to the next aspect of alignment with joy, which is our thoughts. Are your words dressing thoughts in joy, or have you given that any "thought"? Some let their words come out of their mouths before getting their thoughts in order. I bet you even know of a few people like this in your life. I know a few people like this, and I also know a good deal of people who have made it a habit to pause and take a moment to think before they speak.

So what thoughts are you thinking? Does your thought run wild in your head? Did you know that you are not your thoughts, and you get to choose what thought you keep and which you let go of? When we are caught up in a moment of situation, sometimes it is hard to remember that we are the ones who have control. So, let's look at alignment with your thoughts and line those puppies up!

Time for Ponder Activity

What thoughts bring you joy? Sit for a moment and consider which thoughts are joyful, and then list some of them here… For example, the thought of dancing in the rain on a warm summer day brings me joy.

✎…

✎…

✎…

✎…

✎…

✎…

✎…

✎…

✎…

"Your thoughts are seed that you plant"

— DR. WAYNE DYER

Did you notice that as you brainstormed what thoughts bring you joy, the easier it was to think of more and more things? Like your words, thoughts also have great power: thoughts are energy, and you can create or destroy your joy with the thoughts you decide to keep thinking.

So, what do we do when negative thoughts sneak in and plague our minds? And since we are human, and contrast exists, negative thoughts will sneak in. One answer would be to train our minds to see the good in every situation. Now I am not suggesting that we fake it or pretend that everything is sunshine, roses and unicorns with rainbow poop because that just does not work. The is not realistic (I have never seen a unicorn poop out a rainbow). I suggest that we become aware of our thoughts and align with the ones that do feel better, the thoughts that will bring more peace and joy.

For example, during the Covid pandemic, when everyone was locked down, lots of fear, confusion and frustration came with the situation. It also led to many good things also, like it allowed us to finish more projects at home, connect through zoom with incredible people all over the world, and learn to use Zoom. It allowed us to change how we did business and generally helped us to think out of the box. People took classes online that they wouldn't have found the time for before. We spent more time in nature, more time with our kids, and started looking inside ourselves for answers. We saved money on fueling our cars since we rarely went anywhere, and the earth got to breathe a little better also. What good came to you during this time? Did you catch yourself having more thoughts of worry, fear, or irritation? Were you able to have thoughts of calm, peace and joy?

Time to Ponder Activity

The following activity will help you to exercise your thought muscles into alignment with positivity. The more you practice, the better you will become. Try to think out of the box and see what fun and joyful things you can come up with.

For each situation listed, think of at least three positive new thoughts and write them down.

You have taken time off work to go on a 2-week vacation to Europe that is long overdue, but the reservations for your trip were accidentally canceled the day before you were to leave. You now must change your plans…

✎...

✎...

✎...

It is harvest time on the farm, and you are short two of your regular employees. It will now take all day to finish the picking instead of half the day as you had planned. Orders need to be filled...

✎...

✎...

✎...

Your teenage son has decided to play high school football because it is the cool thing to do. You have just been notified that all the practices go past when he would typically catch the activity bus to come home in the evenings. You now get to drive thirty minutes each way to pick him up five days a week...

✎...

✎...

✎...

You have decided to go through some of your artwork to get them scanned and uploaded to sell. You want to have prints made and submit them to a local gallery, you go to retrieve them from the storage room and several of your most significant pieces have been ruined by a water leak that wasn't fixed properly. There isn't any way to salvage any of them...

✎...

✎...

✎...

You have a deadline for work and need to finish an essential report before tomorrow morning at 9 am. It is midnight. It has been a crazy day, and you are tired and ready to call it a night. You go to submit the report when the power goes out, and only half of your report was saved...

✎...

✎...

✎...

You have been doing well and are dedicated to watching what you aare eating to be healthier and lose the weight you want to before your family trip. You are invited to a friend's wedding and reception at a fantastic resort. It was a four-hour drive; you hadn't eaten anything since you left that morning. Your friend was fully aware that you are vegan and promised the menu had vegan dishes. The food is served, and nothing is vegan on the menu…

✎…

✎…

✎…

You are out grocery shopping with three of your kids, all under the age of five. Your three-year-old has decided to throw a temper tantrum in aisle four while the two-year-old is throwing stuff out of the cart. The almost five-year-old is putting random things in the cart, all while singing at the top of his lungs "Old McDonald had a Farm." Everyone is walking by judging or laughing at you, or so it seems…

✎…

✎…

✎…

You have had a super busy day with all your household projects, a trip to the bank, to the post office, and the grocery store with the kids (see above example). You have baked for a bake sale, dropped off a meal to a family in need, visited with the principal due to your ten year old standing up to a bully, took kids to dance practice, soccer practice (were there was an incident with a wasp nest), a piano lesson (that did not go well and ended in tears) a flat tire on the highway, and now you have just gotten home to an overflowing toilet when you hubby asks "What's for dinner honey?"…

✎...

✎...

✎...

"Focus on the good and Joy will follow."

— NITIN NAMDEO

Alright, how did that go? Were you able to find positive thoughts? The more we take time in any given situation to pause and think about what we are thinking and choose to think something else, the easier it becomes. Trust me. When you start being aware of your thoughts, I know it can be a challenge, especially if you are not used to focusing on a better thought. Practicing is key here.

"If you truly want to change your life, you must first be willing to change your mind."

— DONALD ALTMAN

What if the only thing keeping you from joy is your thoughts? If it all begins and ends in your mind, what are you giving your power to, because what you give your power to has power over you if you allow it?

When we start choosing our thoughts to include joy and speaking what we want to experience in that sense, then the mind will automatically shift in that direction of joy. The more we choose what we want to experience, the more likely it is to happen how we want and the easier it will be to experience it.

> *"In almost every case, nothing is stopping you: nothing is holding you back but your own thoughts about yourself and about "how life is." Your personal freedom to experience yourself and life as you wish is not being limited."*
>
> — NEALE DONALD WALSCH

If your thoughts about yourself and how life is are the only thing holding you back. You can change that outcome! There is that responsibility again! How empowering is the thought that you have complete control.

Time to Pause Activity

The following process comes from Abraham-Hicks's book Ask and it is Given (page 231). It is one of the processes I learned when getting certified through the Quantum Success Coaching Academy. It is called Which thought feels better. This process works best when you can sit and write down your thoughts on paper.

To begin, write a brief statement of how you feel about the subject right now. You can describe what happened, but what is most important is describing the thoughts about how you feel.

Next, write another statement that amplifies precisely how your feel. This helps to recognize any improvements more quickly as you are writing down your thoughts.

For example, you have just argued with your teenaged child that she makes no effort to help around the house. It doesn't seem like she even cares. So, you would write:

- Maddie doesn't care about anything at all.
- She doesn't even try to do her share of the work or take care of her things.
- She is making everything more difficult around the house.

Once you have a couple of statements, make this statement to yourself: I will reach for some thoughts about this subject that feel a little better. Once you have written each new thought, check-in with yourself and evaluate whether it feels better, the same, or worse than when you started.

So, you would write:

- She never listens to me. (feels the same)
- I should have taught her better. (feels worse)
- I know she has a lot on her plate with school. (feels better)
- I could always sell her to the naked Indians. (giggling)
- I don't know what to do about this. (feels worse)
- There are many things I love about her. (feels better)
- I don't have to figure it out today. (feels better)
- I can choose to have joy at this moment. (feels better)

The more you practice this, the more automatic it will become to find that better feeling thought.

> "We want to say to you that your thoughts change the behavior of everyone and everything who has anything to do with you. For your thoughts absolutely equal your point of attraction, and the better you feel, the more that everything and everyone around you improves. In the moment that you find an improved feeling, conditions and circumstances change to match your feelings."
>
> — ABRAHAM-HICKS

Our thoughts now bring us to the next chapter, all about our emotions. Bring it on!

Joy Affirmations (thoughts)

- I release all thoughts of lack and choose thoughts of joy.
- My thoughts align with joy.
- I create powerful thoughts of abundance and joy.
- I am grateful for the joyful thoughts I have.
- My thoughts are joyful
- The thoughts I create bring joy to me and others.
- I find it easier each day to fill my thoughts with joy.

6

EMOTIONS: YOUR COMPASS

"Whatever we plant in our subconscious mind and nourish with repetition and emotion will one day become reality."

— JIM ROHN

Have you ever considered that your emotions were your compass or guidance system for life? And that they can guide you to having joy show up in your life daily. Regarding alignment with joy, our emotions tell us when we are in or out of alignment. As Christy Whitman teaches in Quantum energy mastery, if we are feeling bad, we are out of alignment, and if we are feeling good, we are in alignment. That simplifies things a bit.

Where are you landing with your compass? Are you satisfied with the amount of joy you are experiencing in your life? (If you were, you might not be reading this book, just saying). Do you lack the amount of joy you want to feel? If you had only feelings that brought you joy, what would they be?

Time to Ponder Activity

What feelings or emotions do you connect with joy? Make a list of your top ten…

1.

2.

3.

4.

5.

6.

7.

8.

9.

10.

On a scale from 1 to 10 how do you feel about your list? How many of these feelings/emotions do you experience in a day?

1 2 3 4 5 6 7 8 9 10

On a scale from 1 to 10 how many of these do you want to experience in a day?

1 2 3 4 5 6 7 8 9 10

How often are we even aware of the feelings we are having? Sometimes we go through life on auto pilot and miss all the opportunities to connect, feel, and process our emotions. When was the last time you sat with the emotions that have come up for you and really felt them without the story behind them? Just the emotion.

> *"A big part of emotional intelligence is being able to feel a feeling without acting on it."*
>
> — UNKNOWN

> *"You are the master of your emotions, and you and only you have the power to control them externally and internally."*
>
> — SHARYAN ALLEYNE

Are you reactive to your emotions? Or are you aware? Did you know that it only takes approximately 90 seconds to process an emotion? Emotions you don't want to feel, you know the "bad" feelings need to be felt to process and release. If not, they will build up. You do not want to keep those! Stuck emotions can cause all sorts of malfunctions for you, your health, and your well-being.

"If you carry joy in your heart, you can heal any moment."

— CARLOS SANTANA

Don't let your emotions at the moment make your decisions. How many times have you just reacted when you were angry, sad, or jealous? Are you reactive? Have these moments become situations that you did not want to have to deal with or go through? When we instantly react to how we feel not aligning with the emotions, we usually end up in a "growth" situation that isn't always full of the joy we wish to be experiencing. It is always good to process emotions and make your choices and decisions from an aligned place.

Coming from that aligned place makes all the difference in experiencing joy daily. Instead of getting angry and having that energy build, pausing and getting curious about why and where the emotion is coming from can make for a much more pleasant scenario. We always get to choose. And when we choose, we have not given away our personal power. Joy really is an inside job.

> *"No matter the feeling, you can transform the energy of your emotions into your power."*
>
> — **MATTHEW DONNELLY**

"Carrie, what if I am feeling down? And can't seem to find my joy?" If you are feeling down, sad bored, frustrated, angry/hangry, or any of the "negative" emotions, then sitting, feeling them without the story and processing them is crucial. Here is where your freewill comes into play. Choose to bring in a different feeling as we did in chapter two when we brought in the feeling of joy. Express that emotion of joy you bring in by hugging someone, petting the dog, kissing the cat… okay maybe not kissing the cat. Go outside in nature and imagine sharing the feeling of joy with the trees, listen to or sing your favorite song, or thing of things you are grateful for.

Revisit your list of what brings you joy that you created in chapter one. Can you add more to that list? Has the list changed in any way? Feeling joy releases dopamine and serotonin, the happy hormones. We all desire more happiness and joy in our lives.

> *"It is not joy that makes us grateful. It is gratitude that makes us joyful."*
>
> — ANONYMOUS

So, let us focus a bit on gratitude. Years ago, my sister suggested that I keep a gratitude journal when I was going through a rough time in my life, which was great advice. Still, I found myself just rushing through making my list of five to ten things I was grateful for and by the end of the first week, I was not enjoying the process at all. Over the years, I ended up with quite a few gratitude journals that were half full or less. Can you relate? I didn't feel I was getting much out of making a list. So, I changed it up. I would pick just one thing I was grateful for and then list five to ten reasons why I was grateful for it. Sitting and considering why I was grateful helped me feel the emotion behind the gratitude and it made all the difference.

For example, if I listed that I was grateful for the poison oak I ended up with while clearing underbrush in the yard (yes, this happened), seriously, my reasons for being grateful were:

1. Everyone is now afraid of my shower scrubby, the joy of my shower scrubby!
2. I am enjoying my personal space; you know, my safety circle.
3. My husband has more opportunity to help with his aging mother since she is highly allergic to poison oak, and what joy I experienced watching the two of them together bonding in a way that they hadn't before.

Do you get the idea? Now it is your turn...

Time to Ponder Activity

What is one thing you are grateful for today?...

✎...

Now list at least five reasons you are grateful for that one thing...

1.

2.

3.

4.

5.

This activity help you to go deeper and experience gratitude more completely.

Joy Affirmations (emotions)

- I am grateful for experiencing joy daily
- I embrace joy in my fife
- My life is joyous, and I feel it deeply in my heart
- Every day in every way, my life is more and more joy-filled
- I am open to feeling joy daily

"Sometimes your joy is the source of your smile, but sometimes your smile can be the source of your joy."

— THICH NHAT HANH

"Thought by itself has no power. It is only your belief in a thought that gives it life."

— MOOJI

Now that we have dug a little deeper on having our thoughts aligned with joy, let us move on to how we need to align our beliefs.

7

WHAT DO YOU BELIEVE?

"A belief system is nothing more than a thought you've thought over and over again."

— **WAYNE W DYER**

In this chapter, we will really go deeper into your beliefs around having and experiencing joy in your life on a regular basis. Who doesn't want to have more joy in their lives?

Are you waiting for something outside of yourself to make you happy or bring you the joy you desire? For example, when you say or think things like, "When I have the money, or have more money," "When I am driving the better car," "When I am in the perfect relationship," "When I get the promotion at work," or

"When I have a child," all of these are putting your joy, happiness and ultimately your personal power outside of yourself.

Consider this fact: thinking this way will only bring you disappointment and frustration in your joy journey. We do not want more disappointment and frustration in our lives! I would think not; I know I would like to experience these less often in my life and when they do show up being able to process and release them with ease. Contrast will happen in our lives we are all human, but we do get to choose how we respond.

Time to Ponder Activity

Let us look at what you believe regarding your Joy. Answer each question by being completely honest with yourself…

Do you believe that you are one hundred percent responsible for your happiness and joy?

✎…

Do you believe it is possible for you to experience joy daily, or is that something that only happens for others?

✎…

Do you believe it is hard to experience joy daily?

✎…

Do you believe joy is something outside of yourself?

✎...

Do you believe that you deserve to have joy in your life regularly?

✎...

Do you believe you higher self or God/Divine/Source can inspire you to create joy?

✎...

Do you believe that joy is something that will come some other time in the future?

✎...

Do you believe joy is abundant in your world? Or in the world around you?

✎...

Who do you believe you have to be to enjoy a more joy-filled life?

✎...

> *"Belief creates the actual fact."*
>
> — **WILLIAM JAMES**

As you review your answers, you will see where you might be having some limiting beliefs. These limiting beliefs will keep you from the alignment with joy that you desire to experience.

Your belief system can measure your opportunity to have that life filled with joy. What you believe creates your reality in every aspect of your life. So, what will it take to believe you can have a joy-filled life and experience that joy daily?

Let's go into the garden. Yes, I know you are thinking, "Carrie isn't this chapter about beliefs" What are we doing in the garden?" well, yes, it is about our beliefs. Bear with me for just a moment. Cone on, just humor me...

You have a large garden area with many beds for you to plant in. There are seeds you want to plant and seeds that others have planted. You water and fertilize the garden beds, and everything starts to grow. The rains come and go, and the sun helps everything to grow, yes everything. As time passes and you come and go in the garden, you see tons of beautiful plants growing, then you look closer, and you notice that more weeds are growing than "good" plants. These weeds are choking out and stunting the growth of the plants you want in the garden. (Note the definition of a weed is any plant you do not want to grow in an area).

So, gosh darn it, now we have weeds in your garden. If you let the weeds remain, they will affect the growth of the "good" plants, the ones you really want to be growing. You now have a choice to either cut them down or pull them out.

Which will you do? If you cut them down, the roots will remain and will continue to steal the nutrients that the good plants need, and the weed will continue to grow. If you pull out the weeds, they can no longer affect the "good" plants...

- The garden is your belief system
- The seeds are desires and goals
- The water and fertilizer are your words/thoughts/emotions
- The rain and sun, the weather is life's circumstances
- The weeds are limiting beliefs that do not serve your higher good

Just like this garden, your life will have "weeds" or limiting beliefs pop up and these will take from your joy. Now cutting down the "weeds is much faster than pulling them, but faster is not better or as effective in getting rid of the limiting beliefs. It is only a bandage that temporarily makes it look or seem better.

> *"You have the power in the present moment to change limiting beliefs and consciously plant seeds for the future of your choosing. As you change your mind, you change your experience."*
>
> — SERGE KING

Time to Ponder Activity

What are your limiting beliefs about experiencing joy daily? Make you list here…

Example: Only people with lots of money have joy daily

✎…

✎…

✎…

✎…

✎…

> *"You are just suffering from the belief that there is something missing in your life. In reality, you always have what you need."*
>
> — BYRON KATIE

Now to pull those pesky limiting beliefs by their roots, let's choose the beliefs you would rather have. Remember, a belief is just a thought you keep thinking and then decide to take as a fact.

List your new joy-filled beliefs here. After you have made your list look for the reason they are true…

Example: I find joy in a variety of ways daily

✎…

✎…

✎…

✎…

> *"Taking responsibility for your beliefs and judgments gives you the power to change them."*
>
> — BYRON KATIE

> *"If you are going for a major change in your life, you will want to change those beliefs that kept you from having it in the past."*
>
> — ORIN

"Joy is what happens to us when we allow ourselves to recognize how good things really are."

— MARIANNE WILLIAMSON

Joy Affirmations (beliefs/perspectives)

- I experience joy effortlessly
- I enjoy the habit of joy
- I am a joy sharer
- Joy shows up for me in fun and unexpected ways
- I find joy in any situation

8

READY, SET, AND GO...

This Chapter is all about aligning your actions with joy. So let us get this party started.

> *"Joy does not simply happen to us We have to choose joy and keep choosing it every day."*
>
> — HENRI J.M. NOUWEN

> *"There is more pleasure in the process of doing something than in the finished product."*
>
> — SANNETTIE

The final aspect of aligning with you joy is action! Are you ready and open to receiving the joy you desire?

Aligning with our action means following inspiration when it comes, listening to your higher self? Where does joy rank on your priority list? Do you have an extra hour or even thirty minutes in your day for joy? Most people spend four hours a day on devices. Could you use part of that time? If it is important to you, I bet you can.

Think of the most joy-filled person you know… What do they do that is different than the average Joe?

Here is a list of some of the aspects my clients believe joyful people have, in no particular order:

- Good listener
- Visionary
- Forward focused
- Walk their talk
- Honor and care for themselves
- Compassion for others grateful
- Centered/grounded
- Generous
- Authentic and genuine
- Laugh often
- Self-aware
- Love and appreciate the little things
- Don't let the past dictate their future
- Forgiving optimistic

- Able to process their emotions
- Been through a ton of crap and know how to appreciate things

What can you add to this list?

✎...

✎...

✎...

What actions can you take to be that joy-filled person?

Here are just a few suggestions:

1. Do what makes you happy

> This seems simple, but you would be surprised at how many people aren't sure what makes them happy or what brings happiness. Sitting and brainstorming with someone can be helpful in starting a good list of things you know, you enjoy, and even some new things you might try. Example: singing in the rain, dressing in your favorite clothes more often or eating cheesecake.

2. Find Purpose

What do you find purpose in doing? What are you genuinely passionate about? Dot that! When you are passionate about something, you tend to put your whole heart and soul into it. Create a list of what you find purpose and passion in, for example, volunteering at a local children's hospital, teaching yoga, or even cleaning up our beaches to save sea turtles.

3. Gratitude

We discussed gratitude in an earlier chapter, but here we are acting with gratitude. How can you show someone gratitude? What are three ways you can create joy by showing gratitude? For example, writing a note, sharing your cheesecake with a neighbor who brought you soup when you were sick, or even just sharing a smile with a stranger in the grocery store.

4. Relationships

Surrounding yourself with those people that are most like wo you want to become can bring you joy. They say if you're going to learn how to be rich, you associate yourself with those who know how or are rich. If you are going to be joyful the hang out with joyful people.

5. Goals

If you feel a bit like you are stuck in a rut, then set a new goal. Set a goal, make a plan that is out of your comfort zone and exciting to you. No sense in setting goals that make you grumpy!

6. Forgiveness

Forgiveness is not for the other person; it is setting you free. Forgiving others and forgive yourself. You can always call in the feeling of compassion also. Healing the hurts of life through forgiveness allows you to live with more joy.

7. Laughter

Go and look in a mirror and just laugh! Try a variety of laughs, like a big belly laugh, a snorting laugh, a little giggle, or a hyena laugh. It is even more fun when you do it with someone. This helps relieve any tension or stress and opens you up to joy. Have you ever tried Laughter Yoga?

8. Nature

Go outside! Yes, that is where the nature is; go and look. I promise you it is outside. We as a culture spend too much time in front of the computer screen and couped up inside. When was the last time you went for a long walk by the lake or jumped in those muddy puddles (or repeatedly said muddy puddles in a British accent)? What about dancing in the rain or a sprinkler if it isn't raining out or just smelled the roses, unless you are allergic.

9. Be Yourself

Joy is who your creator designed you to be! Life happens and sometimes we forget to be ourselves to be who we think everyone else needs us to be. Stop and be present with yourself. Feel the joy that is within you. Who is the authentic you? What makes you tick?

10. Service or Random Acts of Kindness

Have you ever" paid it forward"? Serving others with no thought of what you will get from it can bring great joy. We have made it a habit of "paying it forward" anytime we go through a drive-thru restaurant. It not only brings joy because someone was surprised by the gift, but it also has taught the children the value of random acts of kindness.

"Since you get more joy out of giving, you should put a good deal of thought into the happiness you are able to give."

— ELEANOR ROOSEVELT

11. Meditation

Meditation can come in many different forms, from sitting with your eyes closed to a slow contemplative walk in nature. Maybe for you, it looks like praying. Either eay, meditation helps us be present and reconnect with our higher self, God/Divine/Source, whatever you choose to call it. And Source wants more for us than we want for ourselves. Meditation allows for inspiration to come more quickly.

What other actions can you think of?

✎...

✎...

✎...

"Power comes from living in the present moment, where you can take action and create the future."

— ORIN

Now that we have our joy in action, the key to success is accountability! When we are accountable to someone else, we are more than likely to have great success. Having success with reclaiming your joy daily is fantastic.

Who will be your accountability buddy? Who is in your joy tribe? We would love to have you be part of ours! You can find us on Facebook at The Joy Tribe. www.facebook.com/groups/thejtribe

9

WRAPPING IT UP WITH A BOW!

What a journey we have taken together! Congrats on investing in yourself. We have covered what, who, why, when and how of reclaiming your joy in our time together.

Now that you are aware of the five aspects of aligning with joy, you can choose to change from that point of consciousness.

Don't beat yourself up if you feel you are falling short of your goals; you are in the process of pivoting into your new joy-filled life. And you are doing a great joy! Get rid of the things that don't serve you anymore and choose to be that joy-filled person you desire to be. Make sure to acknowledge the successes you have in this journey. You have the knowledge and tools now to move forward each day, choosing joy.

Being in alignment with you joy enables you to experience it every day!

- How are you going to create, receive and share joy today?
- What new words are you going to use?
- What new thoughts are you choosing to think?
- What emotions/feelings are you going to process and express?
- What old beliefs are you replacing with new joyful beliefs?
- What joyful actions are going to be filling your moments now?

Remember what you focus on expands. Deciding each morning to fill your day with joy is the best way to start.

Joy is in great abundance in this magnificent universe!

10

SHARING JOY

This next chapter answers the question, "When is a time you felt complete joy? Or what is your favorite experience with feeling joy?" This chapter is a collection of joy experiences to inspire and uplift. Enjoy!

> *"To get the full value of joy, you must have someone to divide it with."*
>
> — MARK TWAIN

Brigitta

When I think of joy, I think of Italy. Everything about this county makes me happy: the language, the food, the people, the landscape. I have been there four times so far, and every single time, from the moment I stepped off the plane, it felt like I was plugged into a "Joy Socket" I felt my vibration rise, and I had the best holidays ever.

There is one particular experience that has stayed with me as the highlight of all my Italian adventures. I spent a few days in beautiful Florence with my dear friend Elisabetta. I had been looking forward to this trip for months as we had bought tickets to see my favorite Italian singer, Tiziano Ferro in concert. On the evening of the concert, the stadium was packed with people. You could feel the high vibrations of excitement, joy and love in the air. People young and young at heart were smiling, singing, and chatting in joyous anticipation. To me it felt like being in a dream... a few minutes away from seeing my favorite singer in this enchanting city that is Florence with my sweet friend by my side. From the moment he stepped on stage, the high vibrations were raised another notch. The love and appreciation directed at him by the adoring crowd and him channeling it straight back at the audience was an unforgettable experience. I found myself singing at the top of my lungs with tears in my eyes and feeling immensely grateful for the gifts of joy and love that I was experiencing. Thank you, universe for this unforgettable experience, and that you, my dear Carrie for allowing me to share my joy story here.

Daphne

My most joyful experience was when I gave birth to all my kids. They were definitely my "bundles of Joy!" However, what was especially joyful was fiving birth to my "homeboys" at home despite having had a VBAC previously. It had been a long and extensive search to find a midwife who would even do VBAC births at home because there was a lot of fear and controversy surrounding VBAC home births. During my last home birth, the joy I felt being supported by a network of women caregivers consisting of my midwife, the midwife's assistant, the midwife's assistant's assistant, my doula and the doula's assistant, was so empowering because there was so much feminine energy present.

Robyn

I feel that a time I have felt joy the most is when I feel completely fulfilled. The obvious answer would be the birth of my children. There is an overwhelming sense of joy and love there. But the thought that keeps coming to mind is more a sense of growth. I feel joy when I am learning, growing and expanding my knowledge and personal well-being.

Donna

Joy-Stepfathers I was blessed to have an amazing man come into my life when I was 44 years old, my stepfather, Jack. He was the person I could laugh with, cry with, and have the best conversations with about anything or nothing. He was the father I believe we all dream of having in our growing up years. Even though my sons were grown when he came into my life and I had grandsons, he became my dad, daddy, confidant. He passed away 4 years ago, but he is always with me and still brings joy into my life every day.

Tracie

Sitting on a rock in the mountains next to a river of running water. That is where I find my joy.

Emory

My joy experience would be when my mom came up to Alaska to visit and we went hiking/walking to the old missile silos. It was rainy and overcast and the mosquitos were thick. We used lots of repellant. We laughed and talked about old times before dad passed away. I felt so much joy knowing how loved and cared for I am by my parents whether they are with me or far away. Joy is love I believe.

Ginny

I experience joy in finding dead people. Yes, dead people. Genealogy has been my passion for years. The joy I felt when finally finding out who my great grandfather was, was tangible! Reuniting families through genealogy work not only has brought me joy but also my clients.

Kristi

All my deepest experiences of joy have been born out of the hardest fought battles and deepest struggles in life where I pushed through until I saw the culmination of my efforts bring fruit. It seems in every memory of joy it was always preceded by sorrow, struggle, fighting and standing in faith for a dream that had not come to fruition yet. When I think of joy in my own life it is always this pinnacle moment after running hard for something or giving my all for someone with the hope pushing me on even when it hasn't been seen yet. Then, there is this poignant turning point where the reward for my deepest moments of joy. Joy always comes in the reflection of the work that led to the victory.

Kim

When I was fifty-five years old my two-month-old great niece came to live with me and when she was placed in my arms I was overwhelmed with joy. She recently turned eight and still brings joy to my life every day.

Celeste

You ask, "What is my most joyful experience?" That is an extremely difficult question for me to answer... impossible, in fact. I cannot quantify joy in a particular order. There are so many kinds of joyful moments! So, I will share a moment of joy that was unique, a kind of moment I didn't know was possible and never expected.

I had recently lost the love of my life when he left this physical plane. I was in the shock and depths of mourning, a part of me missing. Life was suddenly quiet and there seemed an endless amount of time that I didn't know how to fill, or much cared to fill. One day I was mindlessly sweeping and mopping a tiled room in our house, something I could do that took no thought, required little beyond simple physical repetitive action. I had already swept and had been mopping for a while, when suddenly I realized... I was full of joy! I thought, "Wow! Where is this coming from? This makes no sense." I decided to just sit with it for a minute, see if I could get a sense of what this joy was about." As I sat, allowing and open, the joy grew to the point it made me laugh out loud. So much joy!!

I suddenly realized; it was not my joy. It was my hubby, sharing his joy with me! I know this will sound strange, but I heard him laugh and say, "We did it, Baby!" He was letting me know, he was ok. He was happy, and we had done what we were supposed to in our lives together. Of course, this joy shared across the veil was the most amazing thing! The fact that he managed to reach me and let me know how full of joy he could be on the other side! He was ok! We were ok! I laughed and cried with joy until the joy subsided and I could get my feet back on the ground. I will never forget that moment. And because of it, I have known with all my being, he is ok. I know he loved me so much, and so wanted me to be ok, that he found a way to share his joy with me. And that joy and knowing leads to a full heart and a sense of connection with my loved one. I can feel him and his joy, now a part of me. I feel Blessed!

Tania

to So, I thought myself what is joy and where is it held? An overwhelming surge in your heart and soul, it makes you shine and generates energy, from the inside out. A memory of a time, a sound, a twinkle in your eye, a tear showing great pride. A joyful moment, a wondrous event held in your heart where time stands still and you can come and go through this moment anytime, anywhere.

I am grateful that I can look back through my life at unlimited joyful moments. The joyful moment I will share with you today will begin and end with the sound of laughter and the beaming smiles of my two little boys. A child's laughter, the sweetest sound, a treasured moment, and a tug at my heartstrings that brings a tear to my eye, a tear of love each and every day. The sweetest sound and a joyful moment held in my heart forever. The same sound of laughter with my boys will always fill my heart with this joyful feeling and leave me with a sense of complete satisfaction, an energy that radiates, connection more joyful moments with my boys and their laughter that fills my Leo heart. Joyful moments seem to come from the past, yet I sit here projection further joyful moments into the future, that conjure that same feeling, the same boys and perhaps their own children one day. So, joy for me is an expression of love, unwavering love and commitment to my children.

Ariel

I think the most joyful experiences for me are the births of my children. Each child comes in a unique way and time. So, each is different. However, there are certain things that make this a special joyful time for me. The first delivery prepared me for the other 10. After the first, it was familiar, and I knew the prize at the end was meeting our child. Boy or girl did not matter. This little one was special, unique, and unlike any of the others.

First, I am finally face to face with that little one that has been my constant inner companion for the last nine months. I have not seen the baby before but have felt and treasured each movement. I have watched my body and normal movement through the day change to accommodate this unseen person. I have felt the added weight, girth, clumsiness, breathlessness, and fatigue. But- there was always the joyful expectation of the end result, meeting this new and beautiful human. I have made major life adjustments each day for this little one, caring and marveling at the pregnancy process and looking forward to the birth. Everytime. I am so amazed and cannot believe the miracle of it all and none of the pregnancy or labor matter once I meet this new being.

Second. There is a unique joy during delivery once the head and shoulders are delivered. I was no longer surprised by the Labor process. The work, the discomfort, the unique pain of each contraction and longing for it to be over. I incorporated the mindset with each birth that each labor pain/contraction was one less I had to go through and one closer to meeting this precious human. But the best feeling was the urge to push because now I could really participate in the delivery, and we were within moments of completion. There is no substitute to the unique joy I felt, the total feeling of joy and release, that came when I knew the head and shoulders were delivered. The goal was being totally accomplished. From that point, the baby almost just slipped out. The labor was over, the baby was here, and I just wanted to hold the baby… "gimme, gimme!"

Now, I don't deny that I was fully aware of what would follow the birth. I was not living in "Rosy-land" with no issues. I remembered the sleepless days and nights, the nursing, the constant care and nurturing that would be required of me by this new baby, not to mention the rest of the family and daily life. But I also knew the marvel of the development from a helpless and totally dependent creature to a living, walking, talking, thinking, discovering, energy filled, child with their own personality, preferences, gifts and talents. There is joy in each stage of growth and amazement at who we each become. I have eleven children with similarities but mostly uniqueness. Now they are adults and the joy and marvel continue with the birth of grandchildren. It is one of the perks of being a mother. No other joy is like this joy of birth and following life discoveries. I am forever grateful for these eleven totally joy filled moments in my life and the promise and hope each brought.

Mary

Sometimes the most joyful moments are when I am in that gap between where I am and where I want to be. I start to anticipate how awesome having that thing or experience is. For example, before going on a three-week vacation at the end of the year, I thoroughly and joyfully thought about what we would do when I got to California to visit my boyfriend. He had just moved there a few months before and I had never been to the particular part of California. No worries! With the powers of my imagination and the internet, I could get a sense of what the beaches were like, What the restaurant we might visit were like. What kind of food they served? I could see the pictures—pictures that were so vivid I could almost taste and smell the food in advance. I thought about where I wanted us to visit and take road trips to and I informally visualized being on those road trips, long before I ever set foot on a plane to get to California. I thought about the road trip to my favorite locations in San Diego and my favorite beach, restaurants and shops in San Diego which I had visited many times before in real life. I could hear the music that would be playing in the car as we drove. I could feel the giddy excitement of embarking on a road trip together for the first time. I felt myself waking in the Coronado sand. I imagined eating those amazing pancakes that are the stuff of legends, and how Ah-mazing they taste. I could feel the big 'ol greeting I would get from the boyfriend when he picked me up at the airport. I could smell his cologne in my mind. All of these sights, sounds, smells, tastes and feels in my mind brought immense JOY! Long before the trip even started, I was joyfully expecting so much fun and excitement. Was the entire trip as joyful as I thought it would be? Sometimes, it was so much more joyful than I imagined. Sometimes, not so much. But with the power of my mind, I can go anywhere and do anything and create all the pre-paved JOY I want.

DJ

My 26-year-old daughter, Olivia, is my pride and joy. But there is something about her that especially brings my joy. She tends to lean into her personal convictions, and it just doesn't matter if they're not popular. Hers are often in opposition to other people's (including mine) and it has landed her in hot water several times.

For example, one time, when she was in high school, she posted on social media an opinion about something done by her principal that she felt was seriously wrong. She didn't name him in the post ans kept details obscure but confided in a friend who it was about, and it got back to him. I saw the post and said she needed to take it down even though I didn't know who it was about either. What she posted wasn't wrong or rude or inappropriate but was definitely going to stir things up. She insisted on keeping it up and said she would take any lumps that came her way for it. That was my moment of joy... even though she didn't listen to me, and I was in the principal's office the next day where she was almost suspended from school!

I don't usually care about whether her opinions are right or wrong, or what the issue is at the time, but I do care that she has grown up to speak her voice, stand her ground and not be intimidated. She will hold her ground with peers, anyone in authority, law enforcement, healthcare, etc. I've seen it all. But as long as she is confident in her convictions, willing to accept the consequences of her actions, treat others respectfully in the process, and not harm anyone, this part of her will always be a great joy for me (and just sometimes a real pain in my a$$ too!)

Darshana

A joyful moment is one where I discover the beauty of sea stones and I observe how the crashing of the waves on them upgrades their beauty by highlighting their colors while making them shinier. A joyful moment is celebrating my birthday with my family after not getting together for a whole year and discovering how well all my family members are doing. A joyful moment is finding out my favorite student-athletes have signed up for my coaching one more year.

Karen

My name is Karen and it's been an arduous and rewarding journey to my story of JOY! Like many, I have had a great many trials and tribulations in my life, and some major life events I would not wish on anyone. I think coming from a Generation X (with Baby-Boomer tendencies) and growing up in the Midwestern corn belt of the United States, I was cut from that cloth that you must work, work, work in order to be successful (and sometimes success may still not come). Unfortunately, I took that on as my truth to my detriment.

"Money doesn't grow on trees" and "we can't afford that" were common mantras in my family. I became the classic overachiever - rarely in competition with others, but only with myself. Always asking how I could better myself. I started working at twelve years of age, often had two to three jobs at a time during high school. I missed so much of the fun.

Then onto college whereby I put myself through four separate degree programs as a non-traditional student working full-time during the day with classes at night and studying every other "free" moment for most of my adult life. I worked long hours and was overly dedicated to all of the companies that I worked for. I did it all on my own with very little support – more of a lone wolf, I guess.

I had longevity at each of my jobs because of my misperceived sense of "security" those jobs brought me. Sure, I worked my way up the corporate ladder to a degree but being "nice" and not asking for what I wanted nor job-hopping for better pay/benefits, really didn't serve me well in terms of really "making" it.

By the time I was in my late 40's, I had developed some pretty significant health issues ultimately requiring some major surgeries. I was unable to keep my blood pressure under control. During my life I had suffered many personal losses from the unexpected deaths of loved ones, stillbirths, miscarriages, divorce, betrayal, and financial strife, and through it all I kept working and learning. I will share that I was so blessed and grateful during this time to have a beautiful daughter who did make it through to full-term and is now a thriving young adult looking for her path in this world.

In my early 50's, I found myself in a career field I no longer had any passion for. Looking back, I had fallen into this career field at the age of 30 because I really didn't know what else to do at that time and had ignored the little intuitive nudges along the way. Brainwashed by society along with my beliefs and imprints formed in childhood made me think I needed a steady paycheck for the perceived security that my jobs had provided. I was destined to work an 8 – 5 job even if I didn't like it. As a result, I now felt so much anger, frustration, and angst. My health had suffered an immeasurable toll and was turning up the dial. My heart was breaking.

I realized I could not see myself moving to another company and starting all over again. I did not want to do this for another 15 years until retirement and, finally, after much contemplation and soul searching, I took action, opened my heart just a little and I did allow in some support along the way.

My real JOY started when my handsome husband came into my life in 2013. He showed me such unconditional love and support. We were and are connected on so many levels. I'd never met anyone like him before. He was there with me through my health issues, and he gave me the support I needed, a shoulder to cry on, and a voice of reason when I wasn't thinking clearly or allowed myself to be pulled into lack or powerlessness.

It's because of him that I was able to find the space to finally take a breath, to align my energies, and rediscover my true calling (which my intuition had been nudging me toward for years). I'm happy to say I have left my former life behind to become both a Master Certified Law of Attraction Life Coach, a Certified Desire Factor Coach, an Energy Master, and Author and now enjoy a coaching business of my very own.

My JOY has been my transition from a mundane life of expected "to do's" into a loving, trusting relationship along with a rewarding and exciting career where I can now help others also find their passion and purpose in life. I have become a Midlife Transformation Guide where I am honored to help other midlife women transition from feeling stuck, stressed, and unhappy to feeling freed, empowered, and ready to create a marvelous life.

During my journey, I've met so many great coaches, colleagues, mentors, and friends and now have a wonderful community of support that I never had encountered before. Many, such as Carrie Wooden, the author of this book, have had such a wonderful and positive impact on my life. I'm forever grateful to all of them.

I continue to learn more each day. My life is amazing and my present and future is now so JOY-filled! Thank you for allowing me to share a glimpse of my life story with you! Please know that no matter where you are on your journey, you can also create the life of joy that you are seeking!

Destination JOY – Always a Choice written by Beth Myers

in the Universe, and JOY is right up there with LOVE and is always a choice!

Have you ever felt vulnerable and yet experienced JOY? I was releasing my 11-year marriage to my former husband and navigating the discord with my parents and some of my family as I had "come out" a year earlier. For Christmas 2012, the love of my life suggested that we travel to Mexico to the Camptel resort on the beach. I was so excited to be going aw Despite our circumstances… especially when we focus on what we want and surrender to a higher power… JOY can be found suspended in the moment(s). JOY is not just being happy but being in an energetic vibe that is relaxed in our mind, body, and our spirit as you are being REAL, which I term as Real Empowerment Allows Love. Love is the highest vibration ay for Christmas (the first time ever) and the timing of a magical vacation with my partner couldn't have been better! I was fully in for the adventure!

Despite the magical environment, with the white sugar sand beach, the crystal blue/green water of the Gulf of Mexico, tasty food and music and nothing that looked like home, I felt vulnerable on so many levels. My faith was tested during this adventure, and as I deepened my trust in God and the Universe… The JOY just blossomed from the multitude of unique heartfelt experiences that I hold so rich and carry with me every day in my heart and my mind.

A Camptel is a fancy name for a tent with a thatched roof, canvas walls and a zipper door, candle lit at night with torches that light paths to guide one to the bathhouse and other locations. That's right!! No electricity! No room service! Now just realizing that we are here all by ourselves. Or are we??? Each night, just before midnight, the local military patrol the beach in search of drugs that may wash up on the sandy white beach, with machine guns hanging from their shoulders. It was certainly different and was a huge leap of faith for me!! This began the undercurrent of fear and starting to feel vulnerable.

The first night we were there, my wife had an "episode" where she was experiencing stomach and leg cramping and I walked with her toward the bathhouse, but she kept saying she was hot and lightheaded and never made it to the bathhouse. She passed out in the sand, and I remember being so scared… I didn't speak Spanish; we had just arrived that day and I didn't even know where to go for help. I just dropped into the present moment as this wave passed over her and I just trusted what I knew what to do. Getting washcloths in our tent for cold compresses and asking the divine and our angels for help. I held her as I looked up at the beautiful starlit sky with trillions of bright stars praying for wellness as my love rested in the cool sand at 3:00 am in the wee hours of the morning with no one in sight. Having survived this magical night of healing, my partner came to and was fine after that.

The rest of the trip and experience was the most JOY-filled vacation I have ever had after surrendering all to being well and releasing the fear!! From playing and swimming in the brilliant blue ocean and peaceful water, kayaking in a lake observing beautiful birds and scenery in a preserve, being lowered and brought out of a hole in the ground (a sonoto) by several Mayan men to descend into the underground cavern where crystal clear water awaited to float in a tire tube, to being released zip-lining connected to one another over a rainforest viewing the magnificence of the canopy of trees, visiting and learning about the Mayan culture at Tulum, shopping in Playa Del Carmen, reading books in our hammocks outside our tent with a view of the calming ocean, volley ball on the beach with our new friends, scrumptious meals in the large tent with magical candlelit dining and deep conversations with other guests each night. To top it off, warm towels after the dessert with delectable Mexican Hot Cocoa! The

JOY was overflowing in these experiences, as I had released my fear!

Since this trip, our desire to travel has only expanded over the past 20 years, and we have now manifested and begun our dream of living and traveling in our Rolling Home – fulltime. Over the many years we have dreamed of creating an "everyday vacation" filled with JOY as we work, play, meet cool people with our connections, see beauty in our world, eat amazing food, and have a portable and flexible lifestyle. Each day is never void of contrast, but always full of acceptance, allowing, and adventure!! We created that in our JOY journey of 2 house rehabs, entertaining family and friends, caregiving for our parents, Kim (my lovely wife of 11 years) moving to wellness through cancer, the untimely death of 2 of our nephews and me transitioning out of my 31-year career as an educator and School Counselor to being self-employed.

My business name was derived from life being a journey… not a destination… Arrival Coaching. I view JOY as the destination and at every moment we always have a choice to arrive there… no matter where you are or what the outer circumstances are. Are you on a journey to "Thrive, not just Survive"? Each of us arrive where we are in the moments with either fear of with love, and it is always our choice what energy to release, share, and bring in by where we place our focus. Just like a basketball player pivots in a game, we can choose to that in any circumstance and bring in JOY. Do you choose JOY as your destination to arrive in the moment? You have the power to make that choice.

ACKNOWLEDGMENTS

I want to thank you, the reader, for taking the time to expand your awareness of Joy! And would love to hear your review of the book!

Want to know more about reclaiming Joy? Go to: www.facebook.com/cwoodencoaching

Join The Joy Tribe here: www.facebook.com/groups/thejtribe

Check out other offerings at my website here: https://thejoycoach.coachesconsole.com/

You can sign up for a free eguide 5 Steps to Finding Joy Daily from the website or here: https://thejoycoach.coachesconsole.com/findjoydaily.html

I want to than Karen Shier and Jessica Shada for their encouragement in writing this book. Without that one conversation, I wouldn't have even realized my desire to write a book.

I want to thank all my family, friends, clients and colleagues that shared their joy experiences. What amazing uplifting joy-filled stories!

I want to thank Christy Whitman and the Quantum Council of Light for all they have taught me through Quantum Success Coaching Academy, Quantum Energy Mastery, The Desire Factor training, Healing events and precious one-on-one time. The expansiveness is amazing!

I want to thank all my fellow QSCA coaches and clients for the fantastic journey we are sharing!

I want to thank the DF fifty for being a great support system and for the light and love you all share.

I want to tank my hubby and kiddos for their patience and time given for me to complete this Joy project.

I want to thank my amazing friend, Celeste, that I share many past lifetimes with for helping me remember who I am and what I am capable of. Here is to experiencing many more joy-filled lifetimes together!

I wish everyone of you much JOY and success in your 3D journey!

- Carrie Wooden ~ The Joy Coach

Other Resources

Interested in becoming a QSCA certified Life Coach go here: https://christywhitman.isrefer.com/go/become-a-coach/Cwooden/

Interested in "Watching your Words" video series, its free! Go here: https://christywhitman.isrefer.com/go/wyw-30day/Cwooden/

Made in the USA
Columbia, SC
12 August 2024